ANIMAL ABC

QED

QED Publishing

A is for alligator

aardvark

is for butterflies

C c

is for cheetah

camels

caterpillars

chameleon

crab

D d

is for duck

dolphin

dragonfly

E e

is for eagle

echidna

is for flamingo

fly

frog

is for giraffe

goose

grasshopper

Hh is for hedgehog

hippopotamus

hummingbird

is for ibis

iguana

impala

J j

is for jellyfish

jaguar

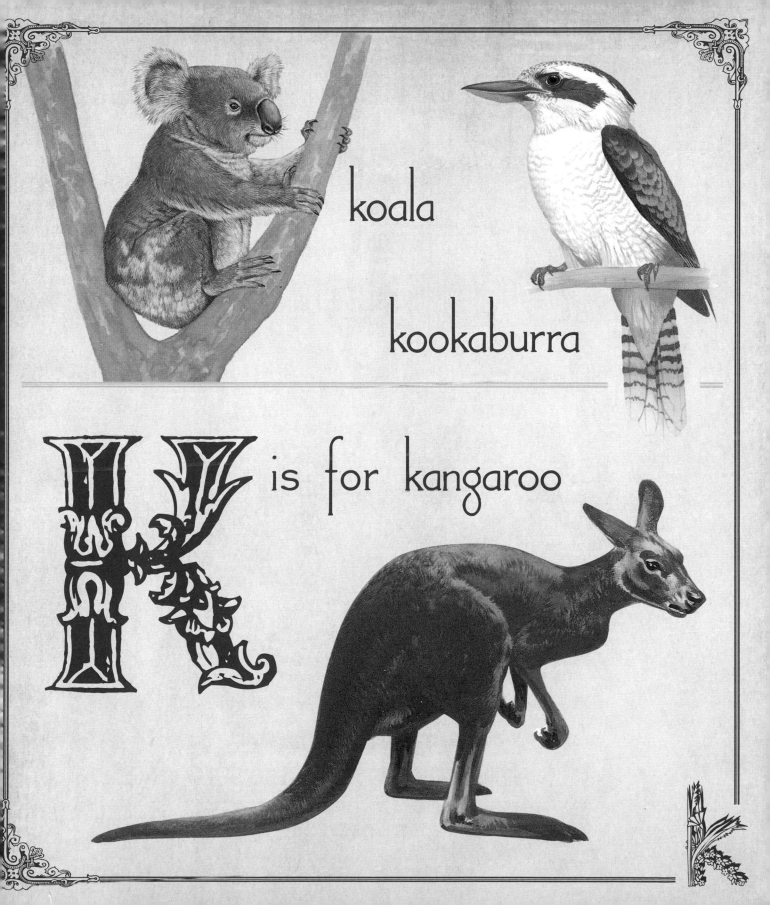

koala

kookaburra

K is for kangaroo

L is for leopard

lemur

leaf insect

lobster

lion

Mm

is for macaw

mantis

monkeys

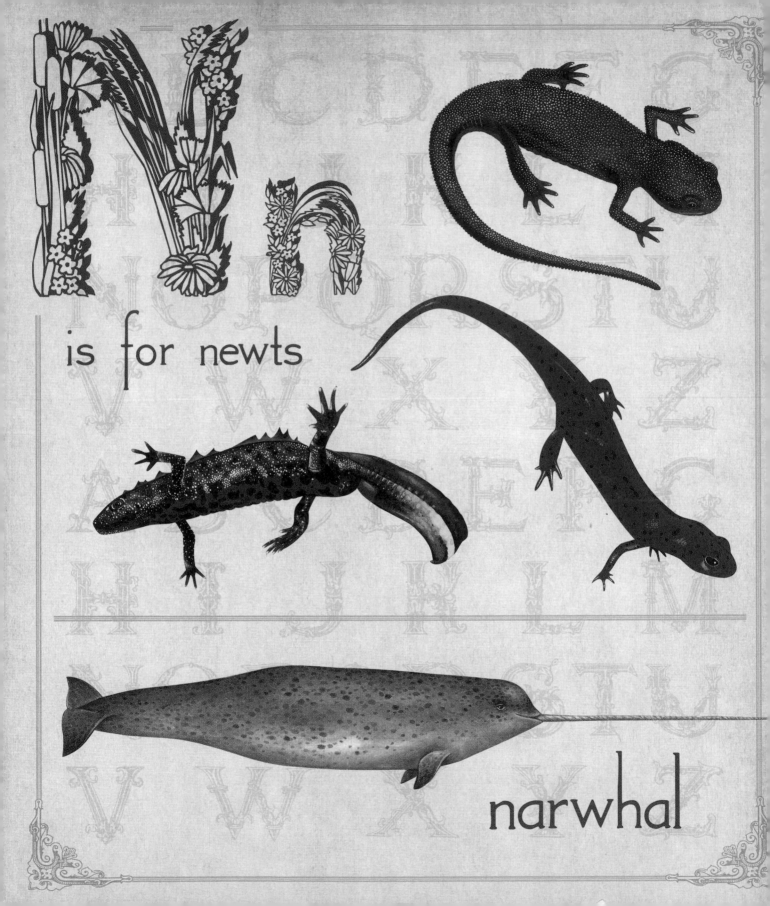

Nn

is for newts

narwhal

O

is for orangutan

ostrich

octopus

is for peacock

python

piranha

penguin

panda

platypus

is for quetzal

quelea

quail

R r

is for raccoon

rabbit

robin

is for swan

squirrel

starfish

salamander

T t is for tortoise

tarantula

toucan

tuna

 is for

umbrella bird

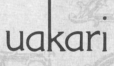

uakari

unicorn fish

is for vulture

vole

viper

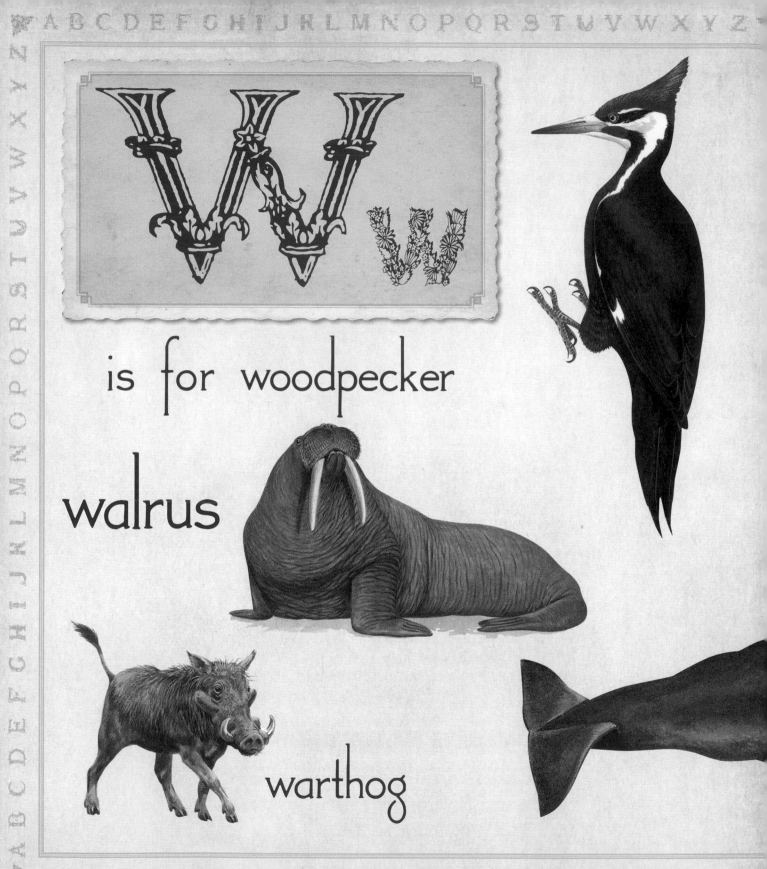

W

is for woodpecker

walrus

warthog

whales

X is for X-ray fish

Y is for yak

Z z

is for zebra

zorilla

zander

QED Publishing, a Quarto Group company
The Old Brewery
6 Blundell Street
London N7 9BH

www.qed_publishing.co.uk

A catalogue record for this book is available from the British Library.

ISBN 978 1 78171 683 0

Printed and bound in China by
1010 Printing International Ltd